FAITH BOOST

...a daily boost for a lifetime of bliss

31-Day Devotional

James Ameh Benjamin

FAITH BOOSTERS…a daily boost for a lifetime of bliss, 31-day devotional
Copyright © 2022, James Ameh Benjamin

This is a work of non-fiction based on preaching, life experiences, observations, revelations. No part of this publication may be reproduced or reprinted without the prior permission of the Author.

Scriptures quoted may be from the Holy Bible, King James Version or may be Scriptures taken from the Holy Bible, New International Reader's Version®, NIrV® Copyright © 1995, 1996, 1998, 2014 by Biblica, Inc.™ Used by permission of Zondervan. www.zondervan.com The "NIV" and "New International Reader's Version" are trademarks registered in the United States Patent and Trademark
Office by Biblica, Inc.™

ISBN: 978-1-958117-05-7
Library of Congress Number: 2022916287

Published in USA by *JATNE* **Publishing, LLC™**
Published in Nigeria by: **RoyalRay International**

Compilers: Dr. Annette West, Dr. Rachel Ogunsanwo

Editors: Yolanda Whitehead, Nikki West

Book Cover Design: Dr. Rachel Ogunsanwo

Spiritual -- Christian -- Daily Living -- Bible Study

ACKNOWLEDGEMENT

I thank God for His call. I am grateful to God for the gift and anointing to be a blessing to the body of Christ in this generation. I bless God for inspiring and guiding me through this book project.

Special thanks to Dr. Annette West for her major contribution to the success of this book. Her Living-Word Ministry has been an encouragement and financial blessing to our ministry in Nigeria.

I appreciate God for blessing me with a beautiful family; my wife and daughter.

TABLE OF CONTENTS

How To Use This Book	7
Faith Booster #1 Poetic	9
THIS ONE MAN	
Faith Booster #2	15
YOUR SECRET ADMIRER	
Faith Booster #3	21
THE TOUCH	
Faith Booster #4	27
BOND OR FREE?	
Faith Booster #5	31
LOVE YOUR NEIGBOUR AS YOURSELF	
Faith Booster #6	35
TWO KINDS OF ABUNDANCE	
Faith Booster #7	41
POWER	
Faith Booster #8	45
RECEIVING HIS GOODNESS	
Faith Booster #9	49
JESUS AS THE LION	
Faith Booster #10	53
THIS SAME GOD	
Faith Booster #11	59
THE HIDING HEROES	
Faith Booster #12	63
HIS RESPONSIBILITY	
Faith Booster #13	69
PRACTICING HIS PRESENCE	
Faith Booster #14	75
JESUS IS THE FOCUS	
Faith Booster #15	79

REJOICE! I SAY REJOICE

Faith Booster #16 83
THE PROPHECIES OR PROMISES OF GOD ARE VOICE ACTIVATED

Faith Booster #17 87
GOD ISN'T MAD AT YOU

Faith Booster #18 93
NAKED AND NOT ASHAMED, CLOTHED BUT ASHAMED

Faith Booster #19 99
YOUR RIGHTEOUSNESS OR HIS RIGHTEOUSNESS?

Faith Booster #20 107
THE SHEEP AND THE GOATS

Faith Booster # 21 113
TAKE NOT YOUR HOLY SPIRIT FROM ME!

Faith Booster # 22 121
MINISTRATION OF DEATH

Faith Booster # 23 127
RESTORATION AND RECOVERY

Faith Booster #24 135
YOUR PERCEPTION, YOUR REFLECTION
[NAOMI AND RUTH]

Faith Booster #25 143
THE FATHER GIVES IN ABUNDANCE

Faith Booster #26 149
RECONCILIATION NOT CONDEMNATIO

Faith Booster # 27 153
SIN CONSCIOUSNESS VERSUS RIGHTEOUSNESS CONSCIOUSNESS

Faith booster #28 159
IDENTITY

Faith Booster #29 — 161
ALLEGIANCE
Faith Booster #30 — 163
POSITIVE CONFESSIONS
Faith Booster #31 — 165
GRATEFUL
Special Note From The Editor — 166
ABOUT THE AUTH — 167

HOW TO USE THIS BOOK

This book has several powerful faith boosters, affirmations and poetic flow. The content presented is ideal for daily use, for group discussion, or Bible study. Before beginning the book, take the time to pray to the Lord to reveal what He would have you get through these faith boosters. To use this book:

- Read each faith booster.
- Take the time to search the varied scriptures presented at the beginning of the devotion and the end of many of them.
- Read and process Ponder This.
- Read and process the Point of Decision.
- Say the prayer after each devotional. Make it personal.

FAITH

Faith Booster #1

Poetic

THIS ONE MAN

Wherefore I say unto thee, her sins,

which are many are forgiven;

For she loved much: but to whom

little is forgiven, the same loveth little.

Luke 7:47

With joy exuberant in her heart like the
flow of a stream is the tear flowing
down the cheek.
On her feet, she runs looking for THIS ONE
MAN who has dug the well of love in her heart.
Seeking for the deepest gratitude overflowing
like oil, she longs to pour her love on him.
Days back, she was trapped in so much debt
she could not pay.
The venom of death saturated her life.
No friends or relatives could pay the debt
she owed.
No one could save her from the dreaded
hands of death.
Eating and tearing her apart was the life
she lived.
Where is THIS ONE MAN
who did not just pay off her debt but overpaid it?
"How could He love me so?"
"I've done nothing to deserve this"

"He doesn't even know me"

"He went into my past, cleared all my records. He came into my present, cleared up all the mess I have made of it. He has gone into my future, made it right and plain when I am yet to arrive."

"Please somebody, tell me where to find

THIS ONE MAN."

Eventually, she heard He was at the house of a respected man known as Simon.

With tears rolling down her eyes, coated in excitement, she took the most expensive of all her possessions and off she went to Simon's house to meet the one who has brought so much

joy to her heart.

Without observing any protocol, she rushes in, falls at his feet and poured her love:

Like oil upon His feet

Like wine for Him to drink

Like water from her heart

She poured her love on Him.

She lavished her praise like perfume on Him.

Those tears were just gushing out of her eyes.

She couldn't contain the love she felt.

She washed His feet with her tears and wiped them with her hair and she kissed His feet and anointed them with the ointment in

her alabaster box.

"If this man was real, he would have known who and what sort of woman that is touching him.

She is a sinner" thought the host.

The one who loves her so much quickly narrated:

"A man lends two people $500 and $50 respectively. Since they could not pay back, he concealed their debt. Who will be more grateful?"

The host quickly answered: "the one with the

larger amount of debt."

THIS ONE MAN looked at her and said "Her sins which are many, are forgiven, that is why she came expressing so much love and gratitude - Luke 7:47.

Ponder This

Do you know you have been forgiven much? God paid the price of your sin. He took upon Himself all the bad that you deserve, for you to receive all the good you don't deserve.

You have tried so many times to love and please God based on your performance and strength but failed. You are fed up. Don't give up yet! Understand His love for you and stop depending on your love for Him.

When you know you have been forgiven much, you cannot help but love Him much. His love for you is eternal, unconditional and perfect. Depend on the Father's love for you.

Point Of Decision

The Father's love is readily available in Christ Jesus.

The price for your acceptance has been fully paid. Will you take what is available for you in Christ today?

Let Us Pray
Father! Thank You for the gift of Your love, forgiveness and acceptance made abundantly available for me in Christ Jesus. I receive Your love and forgiveness today and I declare that I am acceptable in the Beloved. Amen!

Further Text for Study
Luke 7:37-50; Ephesians. 1:4-6,;
1 John 2:15; 3:1,; 2 John 1:3

Faith Booster #2

YOUR SECRET ADMIRER

Many of the Samaritans from that town believed in him because of the woman's testimony, "He told me everything I ever did.

John 4:39

As the morning dew refreshes the green grasses; The leaves on the branches of the trees looking so fresh; The mountains as wet and clean as the dew washes away its dust. Then the sun set, radiating so beautifully around its environment.

All the women and young ladies rise in excitement from different directions with vessels on their heads, straight to the well to fetch some water needed for the day's activities. One of the women starts a gossip: "She will not come to the well like every other woman to fetch water."

Another woman whispered loudly: "She is a seductress; she dares not come around sane and holy people like us." "Do you know she has had five husbands from other villages?" "The man she is living with is not her husband," added another woman.

Other voices came from different directions; "She is a prostitute, a loose woman, a husband snatcher, a home breaker."

The gossip of her way of life spreads around the village. With her reputation and dignity tarnished, nobody wants to relate with her. She lives in the shadow of her past. Nobody wants to listen to her part of the story. She became an outcast in her own land. In isolation she lives her life. Each day that passes by, in the cool of the morning, she will wait for the women of the village to fetch their portion of water from the well. When the sun is at its peak, she carries her vessel to fetch water from the well. She prefers the scourging of the sun to the lashing tongues of the villagers.

On this faithful day, when the sun was at its peak, the *son of righteousness, her lover, her prince charming, a secret admirer* was waiting for her at the well,

for a date. This SUN OF RIGHTEOUNESS told her all about herself but never uttered a word of condemnation to her.

She was surprised, overwhelmed and engulfed in so much love from this man. A man who knew about her dirty lifestyle yet came in search of her. She came for a bucket of water, but her lover gave her a well of water. She could feel the bubbles in her stomach, she couldn't keep the experience to herself alone.

This love experience took away the sense of guilt and condemnation from her, the sense of rejection fizzled away so much that she left her bucket of water. She ran to the village, to the same people who mocked and rejected her to spread the good news of the lover who came in search of her and found her.   - John 4:1-43.

Ponder This

Maybe you live daily feeling judged and condemned by friends, the people around you and yourself. Let me tell you there is an admirer watching you closely. To some, He is a secret admirer, to those who have received Him, He is an accepted lover. He sees you differently from the way you see yourself. He neither judges nor condemns you.

Do you feel like, "this secret admirer shouldn't see me in this dirty state? Let me clean up the mess I have made of myself." DON'T! Allow Him! He is the only one who can make you clean and presentable before Him. You cannot change yourself. Come just as you are, allow Him. He will clean you up and make you befit for Himself. We are called to reconciliation, not condemnation.

Point Of Decision

The intimate move from a secret admirer to an accepted lover has just one step left for it to be complete, and that step is yours. Talk to Christ right now.

Let Us Pray

Lord, I come to You just as I am, I accept all that You offer me. Thank You for this glorious exchange of Your life for mine, thank You for not counting any of my sin against me. I accept the gift of righteousness which is, Christ in me. Amen!

Further Text for Study

John. 4:1-43 Rom.8:1 John 3:17,18, Romans 5:8, John 15:13 II Corinthians. 5:17-21

Faith Booster #3

THE TOUCH

She became unclean

and whoever touched her became unclean,

whatever she touched became unclean

Leviticus 15:19

Now there is a woman having a flow of blood for twelve years, who had spent all her livelihood on physicians and could not be healed by any. It was twelve years of pain, rejection, and loneliness...

The predicament of this Jewish woman will not be properly understood until we look at the covenant of the law. The Jewish woman became unclean and whoever touched her, or whoever she touched, became unclean.

In that state of solitude, she lived her life. For twelve years, imagine if she was a mother, it means she never felt the embrace of her children. What if she was married? She never felt the warmth of her husband.

If she was single, she had no suitor coming for her hand in marriage. The law held her in bondage until this faithful day when the only thought on her mind was to "*touch*" Grace

Himself; the greater and better High Priest, the mediator of a better covenant who swallowed up the old covenant and its curse.

She took the risk by pressing through the crowd and breaking the law. Eventually, she touched Jesus' garment. She was astounded at the effect. Instead of contaminating the one she touched, she felt a strange power that transformed her. She became totally whole.

She was made whole but was trembling...Why was she afraid? She was afraid of the consequence. Under the law when the unclean touches the clean, the clean becomes unclean.

Under the covenant of Grace, the reverse is the case, when the clean touches the unclean, the unclean becomes transformed. In fear, she explained to Jesus why she touched His garment.

I personally believe that for the very first time in her life, she got a response that was intimate and never judgmental. Luke 8:48 "and He said to her "daughter be of good cheer, your faith has made you well. Go in peace."

Ponder This

This covenant is for peace. I hear the father saying to you: "My son, my daughter be of good cheer..."

You are in a better covenant where it is about Jesus, The Prince of Peace (Hebrews 8:6-7), In this covenant, you are His son, you are His daughter, and He is your Father.

No amount of your self-effort and performance can fix you. Fix your eyes on Jesus. He already became cursed for you. You are redeemed from the curse of the law, stop holding unto it.

Point of Decision

Today and this minute, you can also touch the hem of His garment through the release of your faith. This touch can birth an embrace in you for a lifetime of ever-growing relationship with Him. You too can experience the touch of His grace today.

Let Us Pray
Father, we worship and adore Your Holy name for the privilege of access. We ask that You touch us over and again, and we shall never be the same.

Further Text for Study
Galatians 3:13; Rom.8:3; Lk.8:43-48

FAITH

Faith Booster #4

BOND OR FREE?

Who is the guarantee of our inheritance until the redemption of the purchased possession,

to the praise of His glory?

Ephesians 1:14

Once upon a time, two covenants played out in the life of Abraham for us to learn from i.e. The two wives of Abraham: Hagar and Sarai.

Hagar represents the bondwoman; Sara represents the free woman. Hagar represents Mount Sinai (which is the law), Sara represents mount Zion (which is the covenant of Grace). Both women gave birth to a child:

Ishmael was born according to the flesh, as the son of the bondwoman; he had no right to the inheritance. Isaac was born according to the Spirit, as the son of the free woman, he had the right to the inheritance.

I present to you this day a question. To whom do you belong? The son of the bond woman (the law) or the son of the free woman (GRACE)?

The children of the free woman are led by the Spirit. The Spirit of God is the guarantee for their inheritance. (Ephesians 1:14, paraphrased)

If you chose the bondwoman (the law), this is what the scripture says: "Cast out the bondwoman and her son, for the son of the bondwoman shall not be heir with the son of the free woman. (Galatians 4:30)

Ponder This

We are not children of the bondwoman (The law), but of the free woman (the new covenant of Grace). (Galatians4:31)

You are a son therefore you are an Heir.

An heir of the righteous heritage that is available in Christ. Rest in the finished work of Christ.

Point of Decision

Our heritage is life in Christ Jesus. This heritage is of grace born out of the womb of faith. We are seeds of Abraham; this makes us Christ's.

Let us Pray
Dear Lord, we thank You for the privilege of sonship. We choose You, choose life, choose grace. Help us to live in the consciousness of the fact that we are Joint Heirs with Christ.

Further Text for Study
1Corinthians 3:9, 6:20; Galatians 4:1-31

Faith Booster #5

LOVE YOUR NEIGHBOR AS YOURSELF

A new command I give you:

love one another.

As I have loved you,

so, you must love one another.

John 13:34

Does man truly love himself enough to love others, since the yardstick of your love for others is based on how much you love yourself? How can a suicide bomber love his neighbor as himself? Does a smoker honestly love himself? What about a drug addict? Man is deficient when it comes to loving himself not to talk of extending same love to others.

Here is the fulfilment of the law: "A new command I give you: love one another. As I have loved you, so you must love one another." (John 13:34)

Understanding God's love for you will boost your relationship with Him. God demonstrates His own love for us before we are saved. Christ died for us, and we are justified by His blood shed on Calvary. We are saved through Him. (Romans 8-9, paraphrased) As we learn to love and serve Him, we receive His fragrance for the sacrifice He made. (Ephesians 5:2, paraphrased)

We must remember that "Greater love has no man than this, that a man lay down his life for his friends." (John 15:13)

Ponder This

How does God love you?

He loves you so much that He gave up his life for you. His love is sacrificial. He loves you unconditionally.

Understanding God's love for you will make you love yourself better. Knowing how much you are worth will help you value your neighbor and love them better.

Point of Decision

The revelation of God's love in man will naturally reflect in the way he treats others. Decide to know how much God loves you and see how it will reflect in how you love others too.

Let us pray
Lord, I ask that You flood my heart and mind with the revelation of Your love for me and for the brethren. Amen!

Further Text for Study
Romans 8:35 - 39; Romans 5:8,9

Faith Booster #6

TWO KINGS OF ABUNDANCE

When all the jars were full, she said to her son, "Bring me another one."

But he replied,

"There is not a jar left."

Then the oil stopped flowing.

2 Kings 4:6

There is an abundance limited to the human capacity to receive. There is, also, an abundance that is determined by the Father's ability to provide.

The account of the widow in 2 Kings 4:5-6 conveys this thought: "So she went from him and shut the door behind her and her sons, who brought the vessels to her; and she poured it out. Now, it came to pass, when the vessels were full, that she said to her son, "Bring me another vessel" and he said to her "there is not another, so the oil ceased."

Note: "there is not another vessel, so the oil ceased,"

In this encounter, the widow's blessing was limited to the capacity she could make available. At the end of her reach, the supply ceased. She had the abundance that was able to upset the debt she owed and to take care of her family.

Investigating the person of Jesus and all He has accomplished for you will boost your confidence in Him. Everything about Jesus is in abundance. He gives life abundantly. He forgives abundantly. He provides abundantly. Knowledge in the finished work of Jesus is a faith booster.

Let's look at the encounters in the books of Luke 5 and Mark 6.

Luke 5:4-8: "When he stopped speaking, he said to Simon, "launch out into the deep and let down your nets for a catch. But Simon answered to him, master, we have toiled all night and caught nothing; nevertheless, at your word I will let down the net."

We need to listen and act when the spirit leads.

Ponder This

Are you ready to obey Jesus? Simon saying "at your word" acknowledges the words of Jesus. He was ready to obey Jesus' instruction. Peter was asked to cast nets (plural), but he cast net (singular). He did what Jesus asked and the increase came forth. Their boats were so full that they began to sink.

Notice in this case the supply never ceased, it was an overflow, so they had to extend to others. At the end of Peter's reach, the supply never stopped because it was at the word of Jesus. Whatever the Father gives, is in abundance.

The abundance was not determined by the capacity Peter made available, but by Jesus' unlimited supply. With the little that was available, Jesus gave thanks and fed over five thousand people and there was much left. Fix your eyes on Jesus.

Point of Decision

I have the nature of the Father; I forgive not to earn forgiveness but because I have been abundantly forgiven.

What or who the source of your abundance is, will determine the quality and quantity of your supply. Overflow, or just enough, is a product of your source and your readiness to take what is available within your source.

Let us pray

Thank You, Lord, for the gift of Your love. Thank You for eternally saving and forgiving me in Christ Jesus. Amen.

Lord, I accept the possibilities that are available in You, I refuse to limit You with my limited storage facility. Thank You, Lord, for divine supplies leading to abundance. Amen!

Further Text for Study

I kings 4:5-6; Luke 5:4-8; John 10:10; Matthew 6:14-15; Hebrews 10:10-14; John. 10:10; Hebrew. 10:10 -11&14; Ephesians 1:1-7

Faith Booster #7

POWER

For I am not ashamed of the gospel of Christ, for it is the power of God that brings salvation for everyone who believes, for the Jew first and also for the Greek.
Romans 1:16

Power is made available when the gospel is preached. I am excited how the Spirit of the Lord is opening my eyes as I have studied the book of Mark.

Scripture says, "Now he could do no mighty work there, except that he laid his hands on a few sick people and healed them. And he marveled because of their unbelief." (Mark 6:5-6)

I observed in my study that Jesus did not go into the cities and synagogue with the motive of healing and casting out demons, rather he went about preaching the gospel; then he healed and cast demons from those who were possessed. It was the Message of the Gospel first, then healing followed.

Mark 1:14: "Now after john was put in prison, Jesus came to Galilee preaching the gospel of the kingdom of God."

Mark 1:21: "Then they went into Capernaum and immediately on the Sabbath, He entered the synagogue and taught." While He was teaching an unclean spirit cried out from a man and Jesus cast it out. Then they moved to the next town because Jesus said there was more work to be accomplished

Ponder This

While Jesus had power to heal, the outcome was limited by the people's unbelief. The people were familiar with Jesus. Many saw Him only as a carpenter, the son of Mary, the brother of James, John and Simon. Many were sick yet refused to come receive their healing. The few who believed and came to Him were healed.

When you do what is right, just, there will be some that take issue with us.

Point of Decision

The power of God to save, heal and deliver is made available in the preaching of the gospel of Jesus. Are you preaching Jesus? Then, walk in His power. Preaching.

Let us pray

Lord, I receive from You today, grace to speak of Your goodness everywhere, to announce You to all men. In doing this, I see Your power at work in and through me. Amen!

Further Text for Study

Mark. 6:5-6; Mark 6:6-7, 14-15

Faith Booster #8

RECEIVING HIS GOODNESS

For God so loved the world that He gave His only begotten son, that whosoever believes in Him shall not die but have eternal life.

John 3:16

We respond to the love of the Father not only by giving but by receiving of His goodness. John 4:10 states, "If you know the gift of God, and who it is who says to you, give me a drink; you would have asked him, and he would have given you living water."

If you know what Christ has made available to you, you will stretch out your heart and hand to receive.

If you know He has made healing, deliverance, salvation, prosperity available, you will have a heart posture to receive.

Ponder This

Receiving of His goodness is responding to His love. Be humble enough to know this. Ye shall know the truth and the truth shall make you free, to receive.

Point of Decision

Christ loves us so much that He gave His life, shedding His blood on Calvary. Receive the gift of His love and grace. Be grateful for His love.

Let us pray

Lord, help me to receive all You have given me in the gift of Yourself to me and not to become overwhelmed in trying to reciprocate that I miss has been given. Amen!

Further Text for Study

John. 3:16; IJohn4:7-10; Ephesians 2:4-7

FAITH

Faith Booster #9

JESUS AS THE LION

The wicked run away

when no one is chasing them,

but the godly are as bold as lion.

Proverbs 28:1

The scripture for this faith booster is not meant to stir up fear in you or put distance between you and Jesus. Rather, Jesus as the lion stirs up fear in the camp of the enemy.

Jesus is the Lion who gives an assurance of boldness and confidence. The Lion is a reminder that He is to be feared and He is a warrior that protects and defends his own. When He roars, the sound echoes vehemently in the camp of the enemy and puts the enemy in derision.

Ephesians 3:12 states, "In whom we have boldness and access with confidence by the faith of him." You are expected to be as bold as your Father. Your boldness and confidence to access is a privilege, not by your self-righteousness or performance at all.

Ponder This

You have access to His support and protection. Stop trying to earn it. It is by the faith of Jesus. It is a free gift.

Point Of Decision

I am bold and confident in my walk with Jesus, He is the Lion of my tribe and has so closely bonded with me in love.

Let us pray

Thank You for flooding my heart and mind with the knowledge of You as the lion of my tribe. I belong to You. I ask that you keep coming through for me. Father Lord, on behalf of me and my loved ones, continue to cause trouble in the camp of the enemy. Amen.

Further Text for Study

Revelation 5:5; Proverbs 28:1

Faith Booster #10

THE SAME GOD

This then is the message which we have heard of him, and declare unto you, that God is light, and in him is no darkness at all.

1 John 1:5

A group of people came into the church in I John with a strange gospel that Jesus didn't come in the flesh. In I John 1:1, the Apostle John had to write a letter to the church. He shared that, "That was heard from the beginning, what our eyes have seen, and hands have handled in God's Word is where we need to keep our focus." (paraphrased)

John's teaching concluded in verse 5 of I John 1, that the person he was describing who was in the beginning is God, and in him is light and there is no darkness at all.

The same Apostle John went further to say in I John 5:20, that Jesus is the true God. Remember, John was with Jesus firsthand; He confirmed Jesus as God.

I John 5:20 says, "and we know that the son of God is come, and hath given us an understanding, that we may know him that is true, and we are in him that is true, even in His Son Jesus Christ. This is the true God, and eternal life."

Jesus is God Almighty, the everlasting Father. He is God in the flesh. God took the form of the flesh and dwelt among us. Isaiah prophesied about the birth of Jesus, here is what he referred to him as:

The mighty God… The everlasting Father. Take note of the article "the". This specified Jesus as The Almighty God and The everlasting Father. The indicates the one and only.

Ponder This

Jesus is God who took the form of flesh and dwelt among us and now He is in you. God the Father, God the Spirit and God the Son is the same God.

The Holy Spirit is called the Spirit of God, He is called the Spirit of Christ. The Same God not three different persons. The same God is God the Father, God the Son and God the Holy Spirit.

Hence, the Spirit of God and the Holy Spirit are used interchangeably to show that it is the same God.

Point of Decision

Jesus is God revealed in the flesh, He is God clothed in flesh. Will you receive and live for Him?

Let us pray

Lord, I know by Your word and Your Spirit that You took the form of the flesh, You are revealed to me today as Savior and Lord who took my place so that I can come up to his place. Amen.

Further Text for Study

I Timothy 3:16; Philippians 1:19; 1 Peter 1:11; I John 1:5; Romans 8:9

FAITH

Faith Booster #11

THE HIDING HEROES

The LORD turned to him and said,

'Go in the strength you have and save

Israel out of Midian's hand.

Am I not sending you?'

Judges 6:14

The primary way God expresses Himself and carries out his mandate on earth is through men. God is still in the business of using men to carry out kingdom mandate on earth. These men most times are men who were written off, men who do not believe in themselves and are suffering from identity crisis. These men, when discovered, leave a mark of positive history in the lives of others, nations and the Body of Christ. These men are called "the men of valor".

God places His spotlight on these men in the time of affliction, oppression and hopelessness in a nation, family, community, marriages and so on. God uses His men for global impart. Men used here is gender neutral.

Are you such a man or woman?

There are factors that birth these men or women and attract the spotlight to shine upon these hiding heroes. Factors such as:

- The prayer of the saints or afflicted.

- Prophetic utterance for direction.

- Supernatural intervention.

The children of Israel cried unto the Lord in the time of affliction and oppression and a Moses was spotted. The spotlight of God came upon Moses to carry out a kingdom mandate. Eventually, Jesus came.

The disciples, after being told about the promise of the Holy Ghost, took to prayer. Eventually, the Holy Ghost came upon them.

Ponder This

They are mere men without the Holy Spirit. Moses, Samson, Gideon, Elisha, Elijah, the disciples, and you reading, are mere men without the Holy Ghost. What makes the difference in the lives of these hiding heroes is the Holy Spirit?

Point of Decision

I acknowledge today that it is the workings of the Spirit of God in man that produces exploits. I yield myself as a willing vessel to be used of You, Lord.

Let us pray

Lord, I know by Your Word and Your Spirit that You took the form of flesh, you are revealed to me today as Savior and Lord who took my place so that I can come up to his place. Amen.

Further Text for Study

Judges 6:6-13

Faith Booster #12

HIS RESPONSIBILITY

And Jehoshaphat feared, and set himself to seek the Lord, and proclaimed a fast throughout all Judah.

II Chronicles 20:3

Your worries are His responsibility not yours. Your responsibility is to cast on Him your worries.

When King Jehoshaphat heard the news of a great multitude (the armies of three nations) coming against Him in battle, fear gripped him. This King is a man of like passion as us, he was afraid. Jehoshaphat never stayed in his fear, rather he turned to the ONE who deals with fear. Jehoshaphat, in the midst of this terrifying news, decided to see and declare the power and the Almightiness of God. He declared God's exploits in the past. If He did it before, He can do it again. (2 Chronicles 20:6-12)

God does not want us to live in fear and worry. Living in fear and worry is saying you can fight the battle yourself; it simply means you are resulting to self-help. Each time you turn over your fears and worries to God, you are simply saying, "the battle is yours, God." How do you think God will feel about that? Pleased!

Read what God said to king Jehoshaphat when he turned his fear to Him... "and he said, hearken ye, all Judah, and ye inhabitants of Jerusalem, and thou king Jehoshaphat, thus saith the lord unto you, be not afraid nor dismayed by reason of this great multitude; for the battle is not yours, but the Lord. Ye shall not need to fight in this battle: set yourselves, stand ye still, and see the salvation of the Lord with you, o Judah and Jerusalem: fear not, nor be dismayed; tomorrow go out against them: for the Lord will be with you." (II Chronicles 20:15, 17)

God does the unusual when you turn your fears and worries to Him. Rather than King Jehoshaphat sending the best of his commanders to the forefront of the war, as is the normal military strategy, God instructed him to send worshippers to specifically worship Him with these lines.

Give thanks to the Lord; for He is goodness, and His mercy endures forever. The point is this: no matter how great your problems are, they cannot stand God's mercy, His mercy swallows up problems.

Ponder This

Prophetic declaration!!!
I speak to someone going through terrible times and as a result has brought so much fear and worry on you,

Hand over your fears and worries to God, for he is good, and his mercy endues forever as touching those problems...

God is fighting your battles and He is restoring to you more than enough, the spoil will be great, get ready to gather them.

I declare rest on all side in Jesus' name.

Point of Decision

I will choose God's plan and strategy over my worry and anxiety; I choose to give God the battle today so that I can enjoy unending miracles.

Let us pray

I receive the garment of praise as a replacement for the spirit of heaviness. I embrace victory today by trusting God all the way. Victory is mine today. Amen.

Further Text for Study
Isaiah. 61:3; II Chronicles 20:1-end

FAITH

Faith Booster #13

PRACTICING HIS PRESENCE

In him the whole building is joined together and rises to become a holy temple in the Lord. And in him you too are being built together to become a dwelling in which God lives by his Spirit.

Ephesians 2:21-22

God's presence is no longer located in the ark; no longer on the mountain, no longer in a physical structure or edifice. He is a resident in you (the believer).

God wanted a place that was better than an ark. We make up God's presence in a place.

David couldn't build the temple where the presence of God would be located. Solomon eventually built it (1kings 5:3-5), but that was still not the best place for his presence.

In the dialogue between Jesus and the Samaritan woman in John 4:20-24, it emphasizes the place of worship. Jesus informed the woman that what she thought about the location of worship was inaccurate. That the place of true worship is in the Father and in spirit and truth. (paraphrased) The true worshippers are birthed through the Messiah, the Christ.

The Samaritan woman caught that, hence the reason she said this in verse 25, "I know that Messiah cometh, which is called Christ: when He is come, He will tell us all things."

Jesus confirmed it in verse 26 "Jesus saith unto her, I that speak unto thee am He." Jesus also talked about the destruction of the temple, and He is raising it in three days in John 2:19-21. The Jews were confused thinking Jesus was referring to a physical structure where the presence of God was located. They never knew He was referring to the new temple, the believers, the Body of Christ.

Ponder This

Worshipping God in spirit and in truth is not just limited to attitude, it is more about the recreated spirit where Jesus resides, we are the carriers of His presence.

True worshippers don't go to meet God's presence, they make up His presence.

We have the unlimited God, living in limited vessels but His presence in these vessels causes the vessels to do the impossible.

Point of Decision

Hallelujah! My body is the temple of the living God. He inhabits me and so I am fully equipped to live life to the fullest, walking in power and praise, glorifying him in all things.

Let us pray

Thank You for giving me Your spirit who energizes me to live life daily. I will worship You daily in spirit and truth. Amen!

Further Text for Study

John. 4:20-24; Ephesians 3:16;
I Corinthians 3:16;
Ephesians 2:21-22

FAITH

Faith Booster #14

JESUS IS THE FOCUS

Our righteousness doesn't make us righteous,

rather the gift of righteousness made us righteous.

Romans 5:17-19

Jesus creates the balance to all things. His position is at the center of your marriage, career, ministry, and family works wonders.

Jesus as the gift of righteousness. If our righteousness was the basis of God relating with us, we would have been more naked than Adam and Eve. (Genesis 3:7,8,) The righteousness they created for themselves took them far from the Father.

Our righteousness is filthy (Isaiah 64:6). Our righteousness doesn't make us righteous, rather the gift of righteousness made us righteous. (Romans 5:17-19)

Jesus is always the focus, because of His covenant. He provided a Lamb for Himself, fulfilled the covenant with Himself and made us the beneficiaries.

God's attention was drawn to the people of Israel because of the covenant. The people of

Israel cried and groaned. God heard them, above all, God remembered the covenant and acknowledged them.

And because of this covenant, God provided a man (Moses) for the rescue mission (Exodus 3:6).

Each family killed a lamb and pasted the blood at their door post. The angel of death saw the blood and passed over, invariably, as many who were behind the blood were protected from death. The Lamb represents Jesus - Jesus is the focus!

Ponder This

The law places the focus on your effort but Grace places the focus on Jesus' effort. Jesus is the focus, make Jesus your focus. Make Him the center of your life, your marriage, career, family, and ministry. With Jesus as your focus and the center of your life, you are assured a balanced life.

Point of Decision

Pillars are structured in such a way that they give support and a firm balance. We are not built to stand alone. True balance comes from a belief system, the best belief system is in a person. His name is

Jesus. Are you deliberate about your knowledge of Him? Is He at the center of your life holding everything together.

Let us pray
Lord! Thank You for the gift of Jesus, thank You for the sacrifice on the cross that has brought me redemption and now I can enjoy the fullness of your grace. My eye is set on Jesus, hallelujah! I am His. Amen!

Further Text for Study
Hebrew.12:1-2; John. 1:1-9; 3:1-16
Romans 5:17-19

Faith Booster #15

REJOICE! I SAY REJOICE!

Be glad then, ye children of Zion, and rejoice in the lord your god: for He hath given you the former rain moderately, and he will cause to come down for you the rain, the former rain, and the latter rain in the first month"

Joel 2:23

Fear not, O land; be glad and rejoice for the Lord will do great things. At every point God makes a promise to you. There are two major factors you should watch out for: FEAR NOT and the word REJOICE.

The Father tells you to fear not because He knows there are other contrary voices that will contend with the promises of God for your life. Fear creates an atmosphere of doubt. Fear makes you see impossibilities.

Each time you set your heart to believe God for the impossible, fear sets in, so the Father always says to you, fear not!

These factors do not pressurize God into doing, but it places you in the position to receive what the Father had already promised.

Ponder This

For the father to say "fear not" it means there is the possibility and presence of fear. So, I say to you, fear not.

The Father also says rejoice. Notice the verse stated above. The Father didn't say rejoice because you have what He has promised physically. Rather, it says, rejoice for He will do.

Rejoice in the Lord for you are confident that He said it and He has done it.

Point of Decision

Regardless of what is going on in your life and around you, choose the path of faith in the face of fear. Choose to rejoice in the promises of God.

Let Us Pray
Lord, I accept all that You have spoken over me. Thank You for the possibilities birthed in your words. I am alive, well, provided for and refreshed by Your grace. Thank you precious, Lord! Amen.

Further Text for Study:
Joel 2:21&23 Psalm. 5:11; 20:5, Phil. 4:4, 1Thes. 5:16

Faith Booster #16

THE PROPHECIES AND PROMISES OF GOD ARE VOICE ACTIVATED

Your kingdom come,

your will be done,

on earth as it is in heaven.

Matthew 6:10

When the birth of Jesus was prophesied by the prophets, the likes of Anna and Simeon stayed in the place of prayer until the fulfillment of the prophecy.

"Now there was a man in Jerusalem called Simeon, who was righteous and devout, he was waiting for the consolation of Israel, and the Holy Spirit was upon him. It had been revealed to him by the Holy Spirit that he would not die before he had seen the Lord's Christ." (Luke 2:25-26)

Like 2:36: "There was also a prophetess, Anna, the daughter of Phanuel, of the tribe of Asher. She was very old; she had lived with her husband seven years after her marriage, and then she was a widow until she was eighty-four, she never left the temple but worshiped night and day, fasting and praying. Coming up to them at that moment, she gave thanks to God and spoke about the child to all who were looking forward to the redemption of Jerusalem."

When Jesus gave the promise of the Holy Spirit, 120 people were gathered in one accord on the day of Pentecost. They were not just gathered looking at one other, they agreed in the place of prayer. The promise of the Holy Spirit was made by Jesus and His disciples gathered to pray.

The promises of God over your life remain dormant until you give a voice to them. The word of promise or prophecy given to you is voice activated.

Ponder This

It is settled, God will cover your life, health, finances, marriage, ministry, family etc. The manifestation of His promises on earth and the manifestation of His promises in your life are tied to the declaration from our mouth.

Point of Decision

I speak with convictions that which has been spoken, and I am fully persuaded, as I pronounce by faith God's promises over my life.

Let us pray
Lord, I receive Your goodness poured lavishly in the person of Christ. I am who say I am, I have what you say I have. My life is defined by Your grace. Amen!

Further Text for Study
Numbers 14:28; Luke. 2:25-26, Luke 2: 36-38

Faith Booster #17

GOD ISN'T MAD AT YOU!

To wit, that God was in Christ, reconciling the world unto himself, not imputing their trespasses unto them; and has committed unto us the word of reconciliation.
2 Corinthians 5:19

Years ago, my relationship with God wasn't cordial because I carried the mindset that God was always mad at me. It became difficult to relate with my Father (God). I was trying to please Him for Him to be pleased with me. I was trying to be faithful, to earn His faithfulness. I was trying to love Him for Him to love me. I discovered everything I did was of my effort to please the Father and when I couldn't meet up with all of these, the sense of guilt and condemnation set in.

Hence the battle in my mind: "James! You cannot pray, James! You cannot lift up holy hands, James! You are not worthy to stand before God." At a point I stayed away from the gathering of the saints (the church).

I know there is somebody out there who is still going through this same experience. You are told that God is mad at you. Let me tell you that you are loved by God. He isn't mad at you, He is "madly" in love with you. His love is so profound that He gave His only son for the sins of mankind. (John 3:16, paraphrased)

We are commanded by the law to love the Lord with our heart, all our soul and all our might. Every law is with a condition "IF". Fulfilling the "IF" attracts some benefits. No man could keep the law, so no man kept the law in Deuteronomy 6:5. Not even David, the man after God's heart. Breaking a single law means being guilty of all. The only person to fulfil the law is Jesus,

The good news is that God's love for us is not contingent on our love for Him. He loves us unconditionally. Jesus satisfied the wrath of God on the cross. The burden of your sin was laid on Jesus at the cross for your sake. Jesus Christ received the punishment for your sin. He took your blame so you could be blameless.

Understanding His love for you propels your love for Him. He doesn't love you when you are good and then hate you when you go wrong. No!

Believers! The problem with the world is not accepting the love that was expressed to them in the person of Jesus.

GOD ISN'T MAD AT THE WORLD ANY MORE!

Ponder This

Rejecting the free gift (Jesus) will lead the world to hell. A choice made by the world, not God.

Stop allowing the devil to take up space in your minds, he brings guilt and condemnation to you, making you feel God is mad at you. God is merciful towards His children.

Point of Decision

God takes pleasure in His thoughts of you, based on the provision made for you in the person of Jesus. You will need to fix your eyes on Christ as your Savior and not on yourself.

Let us pray
Lord, I am grateful for all that has been accomplished for me eternally in Christ Jesus. Amen!

Further Text for Study
2Corinthians 5:17-21
Romans 5:8-9
Hebrews 8:12

Faith Booster #18

NAKED AND NOT ASHAMED, CLOTHED BUT ASHAMED

Then the eyes of both of them were opened and they knew that they were naked: and they sew fig leaves together and made themselves coverings.

Genesis 3:7

Naked and not ashamed is a walk of faith. A walk where self-effort is not in action. Accepting who God says you are, what God says you have and where God says He has placed you without trying to earn it.

Clothed but ashamed is a walk driven by self-effort as a result of unbelief. Trying to earn who God says you are, what God says you have and where God says He has placed you.

The enemy tricked man into trying to become who God had already made him. Man bought into the idea of self-effort/performance to become who they already are by eating of the tree of the knowledge of good and evil. The Bible says, "For God knows that in the day you eat of it, your eyes will be opened, and you will be like God; knowing good and evil." (Genesis 3:4)

NOTE the punchline the devil uses to trick Adam and Eve, "you will be like God." You can imagine that such a cheap punchline, deceived man who was made in the image and likeness of God. (Genesis 1:27)

Man didn't stop at eating to become who God had made them already. Ever since man's fall, man is always wanting to perform:

- To gain God's approval
- To please God
- To gain access before God
- To earn God's love
- To earn God's goodness.

In Genesis 3:7: "then the eyes of both of them were opened and they knew that they were naked; and they sewed fig leaves together and made themselves coverings."

The old serpent visited the second Adam (Jesus), in the wilderness with the same old trick. The enemy came to Him in the wilderness trying to make Him perform to earn who the Father has made Him.

Matthew 4:3: "Now when the tempter came to Him, He said; "if you are the son of God, command that these stones become bread."

NOTE: "if you are the son...."

The father already said in Matthew 3:17, "and suddenly a voice came from heaven saying; "this is my beloved son, in whom I am well pleased."

Let's see Jesus' response:

Matthew 4:4 states, "but He answered and said, "it is written; man shall not live by bread alone, but by every word that proceeds from the mouth of God."

One of the words that proceeded out of the Father's mouth was that Jesus is His son and He was well pleased with Him.

Jesus already knew He was the beloved Son that the Father was pleased with Him. He didn't have to perform to become a son and to please the Father.

Just like Jesus responded, "it is written; man shall not live by bread alone, but by every word that proceeds from the mouth of God."

Ponder This

You are the righteousness of God in Christ Jesus. It is a gift, stop trying to earn it. You are already accepted in the beloved. Stop trying to earn your acceptance.

Point of Decision

Growing in the knowledge of who and what God has made you in Christ Jesus is where confidence springs from, to approach life boldly knowing that you are accepted in the beloved. Are you growing in faith and in the knowledge of Christ?

Let us pray

Thank You, Lord, for the confidence that builds up in my daily as I learn about You from Your word. Thank You for the understanding that comes by Your Spirit in Jesus name. Amen!

Further text for study

1Peter. 2:2, 2Peter. 3:18 Ephesians 1:1-9; Ephesians 2:6, 8-9; Romans 5:17-19; John 6:39; Hebrews 10:14; Romans 8:32

Faith Booster #19

YOUR RIGTHEOUNESS OR HIS RIGHETEOUNESS

Surely there is not a righteous man on earth who does good and never sins.

Ecclesiastes 7:20

The Greek word for righteousness is "DIKAIOS" meaning *just in the eyes of god and approved by god and keeping his commands.*

The question is, are we just in the eyes of God? If we are approved by God to be righteous, how then can we obtain this righteousness? What did we do, or have to do to be approved by God or become just in the eyes of God? Especially since Scripture says, "as it is written, none is righteous, no, not one." (Romans 3:10)

Before the death and resurrection of Jesus, no man was righteous in the sight of God. Paul was referring to the Jews in Romans 3:10, "who think they are justified by their own righteousness." Many today, like the Jews Paul referred to in the Bible, carry the notion that their good works and performance justify them and grant them right standing before God.

Cornelius, a centurion in Acts 20, possessed the following attributes: He was a *devout* man, he *feared God,* he was a *giver,* he was a *prayerful man,* and he was a *just man* who had a *good report* among all the nation of the Jews. All these attributes gave him acceptance before men but not before God. He was living by his own righteousness. Your good works, your righteousness may grant you *"acceptance or right standing"* before men but not before God.

God had to direct Peter to Cornelius who was accepted and known before men to be righteous but to God something was missing in his life...

What was missing?

Follow me, we will get there soon...

Matthew 6:33: "seek ye first the kingdom of God, and his righteousness; and all these things shall be added unto you."

Take note of the phrase "HIS RIGHTEOUSNESS" in this verse. It says seek HIS righteousness not your righteousness. Jesus was talking to a group of people who had not gotten HIS RIGHTEOUSNESS.

Matthew 5:20: "for I say unto you, that except your righteousness shall exceed the righteousness of the scribes and Pharisees, ye shall in no case enter into the kingdom of heaven." Jesus was addressing the multitude under the law, and he made the statements above to them.

Let's take a good look at the two personalities mentioned in Matthew 6:33: THE SCRIBES and THE PHARISEES. Pharisees means the separated ones. The scribes are lawyers whose primary job was to copy the scriptures. This group of people was very religious, they knew and kept the law of Moses, and also ensured the laws were kept by others. They believed in their righteousness.

But Jesus told the multitude except their righteousness exceeds that of the scribes and Pharisees, they shall not enter into the kingdom of heaven. I believe the multitude would have said to themselves "then no one will see the kingdom then."

Jesus was trying to make them see that in order for them to be in this kingdom, the kingdom we are in already, they have to possess HIS RIGHTEOUSNESS. Except you have Jesus as your righteousness, you are not part of his kingdom.

Ponder This

You were not there, you were not born then, yet the disobedience of the first Adam made you a sinner. The same way, you did nothing to become righteous, the obedience of Jesus made you righteous. Hallelujah! Jesus made it possible for us to be righteous. It is your nature. It is a gift. You did nothing to obtain it, you just believed in Jesus, and it was counted for you as righteousness.

Look unto Jesus, the author and the finisher of your faith.

Point of Decision

We need to believe and rely on what Christ has done for us We must also depend on Him completely for our righteousness. This is what makes us established in righteousness. Do you believe?

Let us pray
Lord, my heart says yes to You again and again even when I am afraid, I will yet believe and trust in Your workings in and through me.

Further Text for Study
Romans 5:12,19; 1:17, 10:4; 1Corinthians 5:21;
II Corinthians 5:21

FAITH

Faith Booster #20

THE SHEEP AND THE GOATS

When the Son of man shall come in his glory, and all the holy angels with Him, then shall He sit upon the throne of his glory:

Matthew 25:31

In this Faith Booster we will take a critical look at the parable of "The Sheep and The Goats" in Matthew 25:31-46, so we can understand the audience Jesus was addressing at that point.

Apparently, in this passage of scripture, these were people who upheld the law and believed that their right standing with God was obtained by their self-righteousness of keeping the Mosaic Law. The *sheep* and the *goats* represent the saved and unsaved in the context of this parable. Note that none of them were saved at this point and that Jesus was referring to an event that has not yet occurred when he was addressing them.

THE SHEEP: represent those that are saved through faith in Jesus. (Saved by Grace).

THE GOATS: refer to those who are not saved. (Not saved by GRACE) Unbelievers.

A RELIGIOUS MAN minus JESUS = AN UNBELIEVER OR A GOAT.

The first thing the son of man did was to separate the sheep from the goats. The sheep to His right hand and the goats to His left. The separation was done before he stated what they did or did not do. He said to the ones on His right (SHEEP) in verse 34, "come, ye blessed of my father, inherit the kingdom prepared for you from the foundation of the world."

"YE BLESSED" they were not blessed because of the separation; they were already blessed of the Father. They became blessed and sealed by Jesus the day they accepted Jesus. The sheep were identified because they carry that seal. 2 Corinthians 1:22 states, "set His seal of ownership on us and put his Spirit in our hearts as a deposit, guaranteeing what is to come."

Ephesians 1:3 "and you also were included in Christ when you heard the message of truth, the gospel of your salvation. When you believed you were marked in Him with a seal, the promised Holy Spirit.

One very important point to note in this parable was when Jesus highlighted the works of the sheep. They did not know when they did all the things Jesus applauded them for that they were not living by their works. They were justified through faith in Jesus Christ. All they did was because of Jesus. The Holy Spirit was in them, enabling them.

Verse 37: "then shall the righteous answer him, saying, Lord, when saw we thee hungered and fed thee, or thirsty and gave thee drink?"

For the second group of people, why are they cursed? Jesus addressed them on what they did not do. They replied in verse 44, "then shall they also answer him, saying, Lord when saw we thee a hungered or athirst or a stranger, or naked, or sick and did not minister unto thee?" They were not cursed at the point of judgment. They were already cursed because they rejected the Lord Jesus. Remember, I said He was addressing the Jews. They were religious people. The missing link in their lives was Jesus.

Ponder This

If they had seen him, they would have done well, all He accused them of. They boasted in their own righteousness. Any works that is not motivated by the LOVE of the Father, speaks more of the self. Goats are performance-oriented and take pride in justifying themselves by their works. You are not saved by your righteous performance; you were saved by the performance of Jesus. Your new identity in the new covenant is found in Christ. The sheep were not conscious of their good works, but the goats were.

Point of Decision

Faith in Jesus is what separates us as a sheep in His fold. Faith in Jesus is a conscious and very deliberate decision we make in acknowledgement of the gospel/finished works of Jesus.

Let us pray
I declare today that Jesus is the center of all that I am and will be. I am a sheep in his fold not trying to produce my own righteousness but depending on His. Thank You, Lord. Amen!

Further Text for Reading
John.10:1-5 Matthew 25:31-46
Romans 5:1

Faith Booster #21

TAKE NOT YOUR HOLY SPIRIT FROM ME!

"Cast me not away from your presence O Lord. Take not your Holy Spirit from me, restore unto me the Joy of my salvation and renew your spirit within me".

Psalm 51:11-12

Are you afraid the Holy Spirit has left you, or will leave you? Have you committed the unpardonable sin yet? The fear of many believers is like the cry of the psalmist in this passage.

As a young believer, I lived at being conscious of committing the unpardonable sin, which is the sin or blasphemy against the Holy Spirit. Severally I would pray and cry with the fear that the Holy Spirit had left me, and this song subconsciously affected my petition.

Unfortunately, a lot of believers live every day with this fear that the Holy Spirit can be taken away from them. Many live in the guilt and fear that they have committed the unpardonable sin.

The teaching that the believer can commit the unpardonable sin has been a torment to many believers because they listen to the ministration of death. (2 Corinthians 3:6-7, paraphrased)

Ephesians 1:13-14 states, "In whom ye also trusted, after that ye heard the word of truth, the gospel of your salvation: in whom also after that ye believed, ye were sealed with that Holy Spirit of promise, which is the earnest of our inheritance until the redemption of the purchased possession, unto the praise of his glory."

We cannot lose the Holy Spirit because he has promised to never leave us nor forsake us. (Hebrews 13:5) "And when he is come, he will reprove the world of sin, and of righteousness, and of judgment: Of sin, because they believe not on me." (John 16:8-9)

The world is not reproved of sins but of SIN (singular). The sin the world is reproved of is the lack of faith in Jesus, rejecting the free gift in the person of Jesus. The gift of forgiveness has been offered. Rejecting this gift, rejecting the one who paid for their sin is, rejecting salvation. John 15:22 states, "If I had not come and spoken to them, they would not be guilty of sin; but now they have no excuse for their sin."

Reading through John 9:31-41 Jesus once again, addressing the Pharisees refers to SIN (singular) not SINS (plural).

You have received the gift in the person of Jesus. You need not nurse the fear of committing unpardonable sin. Rejecting Jesus is the sin against the Holy Spirit which is the same as the unpardonable sin in the previous paragraphs.

Matthew 12:31 states, "Wherefore I say unto you, all manner of sin and blasphemy shall be forgiven unto men: but the blasphemy against the Holy Ghost shall not be forgiven unto men."

Before the statement in the verse above was made, you will observe when you read through the whole chapter that the Pharisees never believed in Jesus. They never believed Him to be the son of God. When they saw the miracles He performed, they had to accuse Him of satanic power, hence the reason Jesus made the statement in Matthew 12:31.

The primary role of the Holy Spirit is to glorify Jesus, therefore rejecting, or not believing in Him, is a sin against the Holy Spirit. John 16:14 states, "He shall glorify me: for he shall receive of mine and shall shew it unto you."

Ponder This

A believer cannot commit the unforgivable sin. How can someone who has been born again (John 3:7), made a new creation (2 Corinthians 5:17), and received eternal life (John 10:27-28) commit the unforgivable sin? He cannot. Jesus Himself said that we have eternal life, not conditional life: "My sheep hear My voice, and I know them, and they follow Me; and I give eternal life to them, and they shall never perish; and no one shall snatch them out of My hand." (John 10:27-28) Besides, it says in 2 Corinthians 5:17 that the Christian is a new creation in Christ. We are different, no longer slaves to the old nature. (Romans 6:14) We are regenerated by the Holy Spirit.

There is no biblical support for a believer committing this sin. It just hasn't happened. Don't entertain unnecessary fear. Don't be worried unnecessarily. God's grace is sufficient for you.

Point of Decision

Your life is pleasing to God, and this is because of the sacrifice of Jesus. You are eternally sealed and secured by the gift of the Holy Spirit that now lives in you. Live in meditation of the possibilities that the presence of the Holy Spirit can birth in and through you, not in Him leaving you.

Let us pray
Thank You for the seal of the Holy Spirit in me, thank You for the assurance of my salvation in You, I rejoice in all You have done for me by Christ Jesus. Amen!

Further Text for Study
Matthew 25:36-46

FAITH

Faith Booster #22

THE MINISTRATION OF DEATH

The multiplicity of Grace and peace is in knowledge of Jesus.

2 Peter 1:2

I was having dinner with my wife when a song resounded in my mind, and I started laughing. My laugher got the attention of my wife. She wanted to know why I was laughing. I reminded her of when we were both in the same choir and I was always privileged to lead the choir ministrations. I would sing this choir song so passionately with tears rolling down my check, and this would in turn stir up the congregation to cry. The line of the song that came to mind that night was:

> *"Righteousness 2x is all I long for*
> *Righteousness is all I need…*
> *Righteousness 2x is all you want from…"*

I am saying this because I want to draw the attention of music ministers to the fact that they can also minister death to the people as much as the preachers do too.

When your songs are performance-based, it will take the people on a performance lane, and this will result to the ministration of death. A performance (law) based worship ministers death, while a Spirit-based worship ministers life. A Spirit-based song reveals Jesus and His finished work.

Back to the song that resounded in my mind that night - righteousness is not what a believer needs or longs for, righteousness is what a believer is made of, righteousness is who a believer is. (Romans 5:17-19, 2 Corinthians 5:21)

That is the reason our songs must reflect the knowledge of Jesus. Our worship will never minister life if it does not find its root in Jesus and His finished work.

We hear believers sing songs like:

- *Cast me not away from your presence oh Lord. Take not your Holy Spirit from me…*
- *Lord, if I relent to serve you. Do to me what you desire. Take all the blessings you showered over me…*

- *When you come to collect your people. Remember me oh Lord…*

- *Eternal, eternal life, I want to live eternal life God save my soul…*

Our songs should reflect Jesus and His finished work, not the reverse.

2 Corinthians 3:6 states, "Who also hath made us able ministers of the New Testament; not of the letter, but of the spirit: for the letter killeth, but the spirit giveth life."

NOTE: the "LETTER" in this context is not the written word… It is the "LAW." The law kills, not the written word as popularly taught.

Ponder This

Are you an able minister of the NEW COVENANT? If you are, your ministration should be of the Spirit that gives Life. If there are able ministers, then there are also unable ministers. Able ministers enable the people through the Word that ministers life. Unable ministers disable the people through the letter (law) that ministers death.

Ministers (song or word) should check the message to see if it is reflecting Jesus and His finished work. Is your message telling us who we are, what we have, where we are in Him (Jesus)? Or is your message trying to make us strive to attain what we have, who we are and where we are in Him (Jesus)?

Are we ministering life or death? Be an able minister of the New Covenant that gives life not of the letter (law) that ministers death.

Point of Decision

The difference between death and life here is the presence of the Spirit of grace. The person of the Holy Spirit is the life and strength of the believer's life and experience. Go with Him in your walk, consciously acknowledge his presence with you always.

Let us pray
I declare by the Holy Spirit in me that I minister life at all times, and I am a minister of life to all who hear me also. Amen!

Further Text for Study
2 Corinthians 3:1-18; Hebrews 8:13; Galatians 4:22,23; 2Corinthians 3:7-9

Faith Booster #23

RESTORATION AND RECOVERY

And we know that all things work together for good to those who love God, to those who are the called according to His purpose.

Romans 8:28

God has positive plans for you. For every loss and misfortune, God has a way of turning things around in your favor. He has a kingdom plan to turn an unpleasant situation to work for good. I call it a KINGDOM SYSTEM OF REWARD.

I remember a day I returned home from work and my wife told me she gave my suit to a home service laundryman. Immediately, I exclaimed, because I kept fifteen thousand Nigeria Naira in the suit ($36). I hurried to where the laundryman was washing to ask about the money. He completely denied seeing any money in the suit and I was sure I kept the money in the suit. That money was to pay the driver to convey our properties to the new home we were moving into.

I was pained, worried and thinking of what to do to recover the money, God said to me clearly, "I WILL RESTORE!" And I felt the Father saying to me, "I will show to you the difference between RECOVERY and KINGDOM RESTORATION."

He went on to say RECOVERY is getting back the exact thing that was lost or taken from you and KINGDOM RESTORATION is being given back more than what was taken or lost, better in quality and more in quantity. I never knew God was about to make me experience what He just taught me.

The same week I incurred the loss, I received a call and the person asked if there was something I needed urgently that the Holy Spirit spoke to her to take care of it. I confirmed; and this person sent 10 times more than what was stolen. It didn't end there, a man volunteered to convey my properties with his vehicle without collecting a dime.

Invariable, I had N150,000 extra and didn't even spend anything for shipping my loads to my new destination. I didn't only recover the money, but it was a massive restoration from God.

When God says He will restore, you should jump in excitement. He is talking about the Kingdom system of reward which is more in quantity and better in quality. II Chronicles 20:25-26 states, "When Jehoshaphat and his people came to take away their spoil, they found among them an abundance of valuables on the dead bodies, and precious jewelry, which they stripped off for themselves, more than they could carry away; and they were three days gathering the spoil because there was so much."

The Moabites, the Ammonites and the Mennonites came to war against King Jehoshaphat and his people. God didn't just give them victory over their enemies but also made them gather the spoils of battle. The spoils were so much that they took three days in gathering them. Preparing for war is capital intensive and time consuming. God didn't just give them victory over their enemies, he gave them access to spoils that took them three days to gather.

King David and his men came back home in 1 Samuel 30 and met their city burnt and their properties, wives and daughters taken. David and his men wept like babies until they had no more strength to weep. David didn't stop with just the emotion, even when he got no encouragement from his men, he encouraged himself in the Lord and sought the face of God. He got an assurance from God to PURSUE, OVERTAKE AND RECOVER ALL. David went forth in that might and recovered more than what was taken from them. The enemies had plundered other cities before coming to Ziklag. (I Samuel 30:13-20)

Ponder This

Like David did, you will need to encourage yourself in the Lord. Believe in God as He promises to restore all your loss.

God has a system of reward for time loss, health loss, financial loss and so on. God has a way of redeeming the time for you. God has a way of turning what the enemy meant for bad in your favor. At God's instructions, David pursued, overtook, and recovered all. God restores more in quantity and better in quality.

Point of Decision

The Father is interested in your well-being and His desire is to prosper you in your body, soul and spirit. The father has blessed you in Christ Jesus. God wants you to know He is your sufficiency and has the ability and capacity to restore what the enemy has stolen from you. By faith receive the restoration of every loss incurred in your health, in your business, family and finances. This kingdom reward system is available in Christ Jesus.

Let us pray

Father! Much gratitude to You for your provisions in all aspects of my life. I accept and receive this kingdom reward system in every area of my life in Jesus' name. I receive restoration in my health, my finances in the name of Jesus.

Further Text for Study

1Peter 5:10; Genesis 20:1-18; Jeremiah 30:17; Isaiah 61:7; 1 Samuel 30:16-20 Exodus 22:1; Joel 2:23-26

Faith Booster #24

YOUR PERCEPTION YOUR REFLECTION

(NAOMI AND RUTH)

Even so the tongue is a little member

and boasts great things.

See how great a forest a little fire kindle?

James 3:5

Apostle James shows us the power of the tongue by comparing it to how horses and ships are directed. Our tongues regulate or direct the affairs of our lives.

Proverbs 18:20-21 went further to make us know, "A man's stomach shall be satisfied from the fruit of his mouth; from the produce of his lips, he shall be filled. Death and life are in the power of the tongue, and those who love it will eat its fruit."

Let's see how this played out in the life of Naomi. The name Naomi connotes sweetness or pleasantness. Naomi is from the land of Israel, a land favored by God Almighty. God had a special covenant with them. Naomi had this covenant advantage.

Although Naomi was entitled to this covenant advantage, it didn't define her life, Naomi allowed her negative circumstances to influence her. This reflected in the names given to her sons:

Chilion means "waste away" while Mahlon means "invalid" or "sickness".

She viewed God based on her circumstance. She defined God based on her predicament which shouldn't have been so. Naomi perceived God as being responsible for her predicament. Her perception of God affected her confession. Was it out of pity? The life of Naomi was not an attraction at this point. Her confession projected "death", her life pessimistic!

When she was called Naomi,; meaning pleasantness, she reacted: Ruth 1:20-21 states, "But she said to them, "do not call me Naomi; call me MARA. For the Almighty has dealt very bitterly with me. I went out full, and the Lord has brought me home again empty. Why do you call me Naomi; since the Lord has testified against me, and the Almighty has afflicted me?"

Ponder This

I asked myself, why did Ruth follow Naomi?

Ruth saw beyond the predicament of Naomi. She saw beyond the confession of Naomi. Ruth saw the God of Israel in a woman who was spilling out "Death". Ruth chose to see the God of Israel in Naomi, therefore she declared:

"Entreat me not to leave you or turn back from following after you. For wherever you go, I will go and wherever you lodge, I will lodge. Your people shall be my people. And your God, my God. Where you die, I will die and there will I be buried, the Lord do so to me and more also if anything, but death parts me." (Ruth 1:5-6)

Ruth connected to this covenant, she was favored and privileged to be positioned in the lineage of David and Christ.

Point of Decision

The covenant we live in is centered around Christ. Therefore, direct the affairs of your life by speaking based on the finished work of Christ. Mirror your life though the finished work of Jesus. Regulate the activities around your life based on what Jesus has accomplished for us.

Let us pray

Father, I receive everything accomplished in Christ Jesus. Help me to see and know You through the person of Christ. Help me to know your love, help me live and walk in Your love. Help father to see Your goodness on all side. Help my perception of You, to know You are good and no evil is found in You. I speak life and not death. My tongue declares your goodness in Christ Jesus.

Further Text for Study

(Matthew 1:5-6)James 3:3-5; Proverbs 18:2; Mathew 18:18; Ephesians 4:29; Proverbs 13:3; Matthew 15:18

Faith Booster #25

THE FATHER GIVE IN ABUNDANCE

Now unto Him that is able to do exceedingly, abundantly above all that we ask or think, according to the power that worketh in us.
Ephesians 3:20

God does not just meet the expectations of His children; The father has a way of exceeding our expectations.

John 10:10 tells us Jesus gave "LIFE" in abundance. Life in this context is all encompassing. Our focus today is on FORGIVENESS. Jesus forgave us in abundance. We could not forgive ourselves, not to talk of forgiving others to earn the Father's forgiveness.

The law says in Matthew 6:14-15, "for if you forgive other people when they sin against you, your heavenly father will also forgive you. But if you do not forgive others their sins, your father will not forgive your sins."

Taking your focus off SELF-performance to receive, performing to be qualified and focusing on Jesus brings you to the end of self.

Once upon a time, for each time man committed a sin, an innocent lamb would have to die. This was done on daily basis. The death of a lamb on daily basis never took care of this consciousness of sin. What man provided never dealt with the sin problem.

"And every Priest stands ministering daily and offering repeatedly the same sacrifice which never take away sins. Jesus has perfected you forever. For by one offering He has perfected forever those who are being sanctified." (Hebrews 10:10-14) Once He, Jesus, did it, it's never to be repeated again

Ponder This

Forgiving others is not a criterion for receiving forgiveness from the father rather it is an expression of the nature we received. You need not bring your lamb, Jesus Christ presented

Himself as the lamb. And this lamb in the person of Jesus has been offered to sanctify you once and for all. God does beyond our expectations. The Father didn't forgive you partly, it was a full payment.

Point of Decision

In Christ you have been forgiven eternally. You are not forgiven because you forgave, you were lost in sin when Jesus came and gave up His life for your sake. You received the gift of forgiveness, and you were forgiven. Now you forgive because it is your nature. You have the life of the father. Forgiveness is now your new life style.

Let us pray

Jesus, I acknowledge You and the gift of forgiveness you extended to humanity, I receive Your forgiveness. I receive Your goodness in abundance. I accept the grace to live and walk in Your nature. I forgive others effortlessly because of Your grace. I forgive because You have forgiven me. Thank You, father.

Further Text for Study

Romans 5:2; John 15:13; John 29:1; Acts 13:38-39; Acts 10:43; Psalms 32:1-2; Romans 4:8; John 10:10

FAITH

Faith Booster #26

RECONCILIATION NOT CONDEMNATION

Therefore, if any man be in Christ,

he is a new creature:

old things are passed away;

behold, all things are become new.

2 Corinthians 5:17

You were transformed into a new man and given a mandate. Scripture declares, "And all things are of God, who hath reconciled us to himself by Jesus Christ, and hath given to us the ministry of reconciliation." (2 Corinthians 5:18)

You were given the content of the message, the word of reconciliation. "To wit, that God was in Christ, reconciling the world unto himself, not imputing their trespasses unto them; and hath committed unto us the word of reconciliation." (2 Corinthians 5:19)

This mandate did two things for you as a believer. The first thing is you become an ambassador for Christ. "Now then we are ambassadors for Christ, as though God did beseech you by us: we pray you in Christ's stead, be ye reconciled to God." The second thing is you are made in His righteousness. "For he hath made him to be sin for us, who knew no sin; that we might be made the righteousness of God in him." (Corinthians 5:20-21) In Christ transformation comes!

Ponder This

Spreading the Good News, which is the gospel of Jesus is a priority in this kingdom. The content is Good News which is the word of reconciliation.

Point of Decision

Every believer is an ambassador of the Gospel. You were saved by the Gospel of Jesus and given the mandate to make men disciples of Him via same Gospel.

Let us pray
Father thank You for making me Your righteousness. I thank You for the grace to make men disciples of Jesus through the preaching of the Gospel. Grant me utterance and direct my feet to preach the good news. I preach the Gospel of peace not of condemnation in Jesus' name.

Further Text for study
Mark 16:15; Acts 13:47; Matthew 5:15-16; Matthew 28:19-20; Romans 1:16; Romans 10:14

Faith Booster #27

SIN CONSCIOUSNESS VERSUS RIGHTEOUS-NESS CONSCIOUSNESS

He will turn again; he will have compassion upon us; he will subdue our iniquities; and thou wilt cast all their sins into the depths of the sea.

Micah 7:19

Sin consciousness points you to it acts. Righteousness consciousness points you to the source (God). Understanding to what extent God has dealt with sin is understanding how much God has forgiven you. He has destroyed the works of Satan and given us victory. God forgives you eternally.

Let's see to what extent God has dealt with Sin. Where is the position of your sins? All your sins are cast into the depth of the sea.

It was prophesied in the book of Jeremiah, "And they shall teach no more every man his neighbor, and every man his brother, saying, Know the LORD: for they shall all know me, from the least of them unto the greatest of them, saith the LORD: for I will forgive their iniquity, and I will remember their sin no more." (Jeremiah 31:34) There are some notes that I would like to share with you.

TAKE NOTE 1: I will forgive their iniquity and I will remember their sin no more. The book of Hebrews declares, "this is the covenant that I will make with them after those days, saith the Lord, I will put my laws into their hearts, and in their minds will I write them; And their sins and iniquities will I remember no more. Now where remission of these is, there is no more offering for sin." (Hebrews 10:16-18)

TAKE NOTE 2: Their sins and iniquities will I remember no more and there is no more offering of sin. There is no more offering for sin because Jesus has dealt with sin once and for all. "To wit, that God was in Christ, reconciling the world unto himself, not imputing their trespasses unto them; and hath committed unto us the word of reconciliation." (2 Corinthians 5:19)

TAK NOTE 3: "Not inputting their trespasses unto them... Even as David also describeth the blessedness of the man, unto whom God imputeth righteousness without works, Saying, Blessed are they whose iniquities are forgiven, and whose sins are covered. Blessed is the man to whom the Lord will not impute sin." (Romans 4:6-8)

Ponder This

"TO WHOM THE LORD WILL NOT impute SIN". Know that your sin was dealt with, and you are forgiven eternally.

Point of Decision

Sin consciousness breeds acts; Righteousness consciousness produces fruits. Therefore, accept the fact that you were made righteous by faith in Jesus. It is called the gift of righteous. Be righteous conscious not Sin conscious.

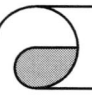

Let us pray:
Thank you, father, for making me Your Righteousness. I am no longer a sinner. I am the righteousness of God in Christ Jesus therefore I live and walk in righteousness. I do not live-in condemnation, I am eternally forgiven by the father. I am blessed because I have the blessed life. I am the righteousness of God in Christ Jesus.

Further Text for Study
Romans 8:8-10; Romans 8:1; 2 Corinthians 10:17; Hebrews 14:10; Romans 4:8

FAITH

Faith Booster #28
Poetic Flow

MY IDENTITY

I am God's choicest vine.
I am God's chosen one.
I am a royal priesthood.
Looking into the mirror,
I see God's special creature.
I have semblance with God
because I am created in the image of God.
In Him, I move, I live and have my being.
The Holy Spirit lives in me, He is alive in me,
I am alive in Him which makes me
an extra ordinary being.
I carry the presence of Jesus with me wherever I go.
I am His representative on earth.
I am loved because I know He loves me.

I am joint heir with Christ.
Even though I walk through the valley of the shadow of death, I shall fear no evil.
I am super blessed because I have the precious blood of Jesus which is a powerful seal.
I have the powerful name of Jesus;
I have the sweet Holy Spirit and
I have ministering angels.

Faith Booster #29
Poetic Flow

ALLEGIANCE

I pledge allegiance to the Almighty.
To love Him, with all of my heart
all of my soul and
all of my strength
None of self and all of Him.
I seek to honor and obey Him.
In my life (spiritual, physical, marital, social)
God will be glorified.
My life will draw men unto Him.
I have laid my hands on the 'plough',
no going back, no looking back!
I will remain in the fold and
encourage as many as possible.
I will be, at each step of the way,
what the Lord wants me to be.
I will treasure and continually sustain

my fellowship and intimacy with Him.
I will study the scriptures,
to show myself approved unto God.
I love my Master.

Faith Booster #30
Poetic Flow

POSITIVE CONFESSIONS

The Lord has made me the head
and not the tail.
I shall be above always.
I shall wax greater and greater.
He shall cover me with his feathers
and under His wings I will hide.
The name of the Lord is a strong tower,
I run into it, and I am saved.
Gentiles are coming to my light and
Kings to the brightness of my rising.
I am blessed with discerning spirit.
I am blessed with wisdom.
I exude spiritual intelligence.

FAITH

Faith Booster #31
Poetic Flow

GRATEFUL

For all the things God has done,
the things I have learned
and the much He will still do in my life,
I say, thank You Lord.
You Lord have sustained and been my guide
every day of this journey.
I am thankful.
I am Grateful for who You are
I am Grateful for what You do
I am Grateful that You love me
beyond my faults.
I am Grateful.

Special Note from the Author

I am super excited that you took this 31-day journey through my writings. I hope you have been enriched and fulfilled. Beyond today, I believe it is definitely going to be a lifetime of bliss, *JOY*, for you, in Christ Jesus.

Let us pray
Lord, we ask, that You will continue to keep us in Your care. We commit to be intentional doers of your word. May we take Your Truth, Biblical Principles and live them out every day.
Amen.

ABOUT THE AUTHOR

James Ameh Benjamin's life is full of active and intentional service to God in defined ministry both to the local church and to the Body of Christ as a whole.

He received Christ as a teenager and launched on immediately into Evangelical messages, with the wind of the miraculous confirming his calling even then as a "playful preacher" gathering children together, in enthusiastic praise, worship and messages on the streets and under any available tree shade they found.

After his formal education where he got a brief training as an accountant, he started a drama group that became very popular with their depth of spiritual delivery full of creativity, comic and wrapped on all sides with scriptural references. O.C.A.F an acronym for Overcomers Creative Art Forum had a very huge share of criticism as many felt he has been rebellious and was about to forcefully take young folks away from their churches to build a name for himself, the name of the drama group was later changed to TREASURE BOX, and it became an interdenominational outreach.

He was called the creative director at this time, but he demonstrated the grace of a pastor, molder and a model to many of the young people God brought his way. As a result of that early grooming, many of them are established in the faith and in ministry till date.

His foundation with script writing and directing was God's way of building and exposing him into the prophetic and Apostolic ministry where he functions in very strongly now.

He later got a formal training at the United Christian Faith Ministries (UCFM) based in the USA where he was certified and ordained as a pastor and has been affirmed as an Apostle with Fresh Oil ministries International based in the USA.

Apostle James is an itinerant minister of the gospel of Jesus based presently in Abuja, Nigeria. He is married to his darling wife, Blessing Onyemaechi Benjamin and they are blessed with one lovely daughter, Thalia.

FAITH

Made in the USA
Columbia, SC
19 September 2022